TOPIC

Can I Really Live in Victory?

SCRIPTURES

1. **Ephesians 5:1** — Therefore be imitators of God as dear children.

2. **John 10:17,18** — Therefore My Father loves Me, because I lay down My life that I may take it again. No one takes it from Me, but I lay it down of Myself. I have power to lay it down, and I have power to take it again. This command I have received from My Father.

3. **John 17:1** — Jesus spoke these words, lifted up His eyes to heaven, and said: "Father, the hour has come. Glorify Your Son, that Your Son also may glorify You."

4. **Hebrews 12:2** — Looking unto Jesus, the author and finisher of our faith, who for the joy that was set before Him endured the cross, despising the shame, and has sat down at the right hand of the throne of God.

5. **Hebrews 1:9** — You have loved righteousness and hated lawlessness; therefore God, Your God, has anointed You with the oil of gladness more than Your companions.

6. **Romans 8:35–37** — Who shall separate us from the love of Christ? Shall tribulation, or distress, or persecution, or famine, or nakedness, or peril, or sword? As it is written: "For Your sake we are killed all day long; we are accounted as sheep for the slaughter." Yet in all these things we are more than conquerors through Him who loved us.

7. **Proverbs 23:7** — For as he thinks in his heart, so is he....

8. **Colossians 3:12** — Therefore, as the elect of God, holy and beloved, put on tender mercies, kindness, humility, meekness, longsuffering.

9. **Colossians 1:22** — In the body of His flesh through death, to present you holy, and blameless, and above reproach in His sight.

10. **Romans 12:2** — And do not be conformed to this world, but be transformed by the renewing of your mind, that you may prove what is that good and acceptable and perfect will of God.

SYNOPSIS

The five lessons in this study on *How To Be Imitators of God* will focus on the following topics:

- Can I Really Live in Victory?
- Are You Giving God's Way?
- Why Should I Forgive?
- Are You Carrying the Fragrance of Christ?
- Are You Ready To Let Go of Worry?

The emphasis of this lesson:

God called us to be imitators of Him as His dear children. This means we are a victor, not a victim — because our victorious, powerful, triumphant God lives within us. When we realize that we are more than conquerors through Him who loves us, we can rise up, take on His identity, and walk in victory in our lives.

In the program, Denise Renner shared a delightful memory from her grandchildren's younger years. She recalled how her granddaughters would eagerly slip into her high heels and wobble around the house, pretending to be just like her. Another time, one of her grandchildren wore one of her husband Rick's coats, acting out the role of Grandpa. It's a charming habit many children share — imitating those they admire. As we grow up, we often model ourselves after the people we look up to. Ephesians 5:1 invites us to do the same with God: "be imitators of God as dear children."

Just as Denise's grandchildren imitated their grandparents, or as children often mimic their parents, we are called to imitate our Heavenly Father. There's a common saying that states "imitation is the sincerest form of flattery," and when we align our thoughts and actions with God's thoughts and actions, we are giving Him the greatest compliment. To do this well, though, we must first understand what God is like.

How We Can Be Victors

One powerful way we can imitate God is by looking at the life of Jesus. Throughout the Scriptures, we see that Jesus was never a victim; He was always a victor. Some might argue that Jesus was a victim when He was

A Note From Denise Renner

The Word of God is so powerful in our lives. It is essential that every person spend time with God and study His Word in order to stay spiritually strong in these last days.

This study guide corresponds to my *TIME With Denise Renner* TV program by the same title that can be viewed at **deniserenner.org**. My desire is that through these lessons, you find the encouragement and freedom in Christ that you need. I believe the Holy Spirit is going to speak to you through the words you read in this study tool and that as you begin to use it, you will be *propelled* into the abundant life God has planned for you. I encourage you to make the effort to receive all He has for you and all He wants to do in you — it will definitely be worth it!

Whether you have walked with the Lord a long time or have just begun to follow Him, there is so much He wants to give you from His Word. He sees where you are, and He wants to meet you there.

> Therefore do not worry about tomorrow, for tomorrow
> will worry about its own things.
> Sufficient for the day is its own trouble.
> — Matthew 6:34

Your sister and friend in Jesus Christ,

Denise Renner

Denise Renner

Unless otherwise indicated, all scripture quotations are taken from the *New King James Version*®. Copyright © 1982 by Thomas Nelson. Used by permission. All rights reserved.

Scripture quotations marked (*AMPC*) are taken from the *Amplified*® *Bible, Classic Edition.* Copyright © 1954, 1958, 1962, 1964, 1965, 1987 by The Lockman Foundation. Used by permission. **www.Lockman.org**

How To Be Imitators of God

Copyright © 2025 by Denise Renner
1814 W. Tacoma St.
Broken Arrow, OK 74012-1406

Published by Rick Renner Ministries
www.renner.org

ISBN 13: 978-1-6675-1243-3

eBook ISBN 13: 978-1-6675-1243-3

All rights reserved. No portion of this book may be reproduced or transmitted in any form or by any means — electronic, mechanical, photocopy, recording, scanning, or other (except for brief quotations in critical reviews or articles) — without the prior written permission of the Publisher.

on the Cross, but that's not the case. Even in that moment, He was still a victor. In fact, John 10:17 and 18 says:

> Therefore My Father loves Me, because I lay down My life that I may take it again. No one takes it from Me, but I lay it down of Myself. I have power to lay it down, and I have power to take it again. This command I have received from My Father.

When the authorities arrested Jesus, He didn't resist; He went with them willingly. The Jewish leaders and soldiers didn't take His life — Jesus *gave* it of His own accord. He declared, "I have power to lay it down, and I have power to take it again." No one took His life from Him. Rather, He *chose* to lay it down. Although religion has often painted Jesus as a victim on the Cross, He was anything but. He was the ultimate victor. Before His crucifixion, Jesus Himself confirmed this, saying:

> '…Father, the hour has come. Glorify Your Son, that Your Son also may glorify You.'
>
> — John 17:1

Jesus saw the Cross, death, and hell not as defeat, but as the means through which He would glorify God — and in turn, be glorified by Him. Friend, that's not a victim. That's a *victor*. Hebrews 12:2 says, "Looking unto Jesus, the author and finisher of our faith, who for the joy that was set before Him endured the Cross, despising the shame, and has sat down at the right hand of the throne of God."

Jesus did not see the Cross as a place where His life was taken from Him. He did not look at Himself as a victim to their punishment. Instead He went to His death on the Cross as a victor. He went into it mindful of "the joy that was set before Him." This is a powerful revelation!

See Jesus As He Truly Is

If we're going to imitate Jesus, we must first understand who He *really is*. Many of us have been influenced by religious portrayals that paint Him as a victim, when that isn't the truth. To follow His example, we need a clear and accurate understanding of His identity. Consider the description of Jesus in Hebrews 1:9, which says:

> You have loved righteousness and hated lawlessness; therefore God, Your God, has anointed You with the oil of gladness more than Your companions.

If we had been with Jesus in the flesh, then according to this verse, we would have said, "He's the happiest person. He's so joyful." According to Hebrews 1:9, He was the happiest among all His companions. And when we look at Jesus face to face one day, we won't see a victim — we'll see a victor. So when Ephesians 5:1 says, "Therefore be imitators of God as dear children," it means that we are to imitate Him in victory, not in victimhood.

It's easy to fall into the victim mindset in this life. We live in a broken world filled with opportunities to feel defeated, and when we think on our imperfections — or the ways others have wronged us — we may feel sorry for ourselves. We may start to think of ourselves as victims. But God's Word reminds us, "Therefore be imitators of God as dear children." As His dear children, we are called to imitate Him — *by walking in victory!*

Friend, you are not a victim. You are a victor! Instead of lowering your head in defeat, lift it high with confidence. You may not always *feel* victorious, but the Word of God doesn't tell you to act in victory only when you feel like it. No, you're to *imitate* Him and *act like* Him, and you do that *by faith*. Victory is a choice — an act of your will.

Decide To Put On Victory

So how do you imitate Jesus in situations when you feel like a victim and not a victor? You *put on* victory! Let's look at the real you. Romans 8:37 tells you exactly who you are by saying, "Yet in all these things we are more than conquerors through Him who loved us."

This verse doesn't just say we are conquerors. It says, we are *more than conquerors.* This is our identity today at this very minute — not yesterday, not in the future, but *right now.* We are victors! Not only are we are more than conquerors, but we're more than conquerors "in all these things." What kind of things is this verse talking about? Consider this passage of Scripture in Romans 8:35–37:

> **Who shall separate us from the love of Christ? Shall tribulation, or distress, or persecution, or famine, or nakedness, or peril, or sword? As it is written: "For Your sake we are killed all day long; we are accounted as sheep for the slaughter." Yet in all these things we are more than conquerors through Him who loved us.**

How powerful is that! It is often tempting to look at those who are experiencing what is described in this verse and say, "They're persecuted. They're dealing with famine, and they don't have enough clothes. They are being attacked with a sword. They truly are victims." We might look at people going through these things and say they are being targeted by someone else. *But not in Christ!* In Christ, they are no longer victims — they are conquerors. The same goes for us and our lives.

This is our true identity. It's so important that we believe this scriptural truth. Proverbs 23:7 says, "For as he thinks in his heart, so is he…." We may know this Bible verse, but do we believe it? How we think of ourselves is important because what we think about ourselves is what we become. It matters what we believe about ourselves.

So don't think of yourself as a victim. God made you a victor through Christ Jesus. Your situation may be tough, or you may not like how you're being treated — but you are still an overcomer. You are more than a conqueror through Christ Jesus!

We Are Holy and Beloved

In some religions, there are statues of individuals called saints. God calls us "holy," which means *saint*. But what does the word "saint" mean? It means *one who is set apart for a holy purpose.* That's you! Colossians 3:12 says, "Therefore, as the elect of God, holy and beloved, put on tender mercies, kindness, humility, meekness, longsuffering."

He calls you "holy." He calls you "the elect of God." And there's something else — He declares that you are "beloved." When you are fighting a victim mentality, you might feel as if you are not beloved. But that is just a feeling. It's not who you truly are.

You might have been rejected by someone, but you are not "the rejected." That's not your label. Your identity is that you are His "beloved." You are not a victim of someone else's treatment. You are a victor. The Word of God says you are more than a conqueror. This is good news!

Colossians 1:22 says, "In the body of His flesh through death, to present you holy, and blameless, and above reproach in His sight. . . ." This verse declares that you are "blameless." This doesn't mean that you don't do anything wrong; the Word of God calls you "blameless" because of the blood of Jesus. You are blameless because you trust in the Blood. You are declared blameless because of the One who lives within you. He who lives inside you is the Victor, not the victim. The real and true you is a victor.

Believe You Are Who God Says You Are

We must be careful to change what we think and say about ourselves. No matter what's going on around us or what we are enduring, we must identify with the Word of God. We can say to ourselves, *I know I'm going through this and that, but the Word of God calls me "beloved." His Word calls me "the elect of God." He calls me "blameless." His Word calls me "more than a conqueror."* This is the truth!

Romans 12:2 says, "And do not be conformed to this world, but be transformed by the renewing of your mind, that you may prove what is that good and acceptable and perfect will of God." We are to renew our mind so that, as it says in this verse, we would know the "good and acceptable and perfect will of God."

When we start thinking right, we start believing right. We start believing and knowing the perfect will of God. Consider this statement Denise made in the program: "As we recognize who is in us and who we are, it is easier to agree with God, throw off the victim mentality, and put on the victor."

There is power, not just in knowing the Scriptures, but in *agreeing* and *aligning yourself* with them. When you say, "I am not the victim. I am the victor," then it's easy to put your shoulders back, lift up your head, and say, "I'm the victor in this situation! No matter what happens or what I do, I'm going to be victorious in that area of my life!"

Take Charge of Your Thoughts

It is so easy for our minds to drift when we have to do something that we've never done before. We might not feel confident about it, so we may think, *I hope it works out. I hope I don't mess up.* But if we're going to imitate God, then we must choose to think, *I'm the victor in this situation. I'm going to do well.* This is so much better than thinking, *I hope I do well.*

The Victor lives inside you! You must learn to listen to the Victor and talk like the Victor, declaring that you are going to succeed. Maybe you have an exam, and you think, *I don't know if I'm going to pass this test.* But the truth is, you studied, so you can tell yourself, *I'm going to do well.*

Maybe you're going into a conversation that will be difficult, and you're upset about it and don't know what to do. You can tell yourself, *The Victor lives inside me. The Holy Spirit will guide me through this conversation, and I'm not going to be the victim. I am the victor through Christ Jesus.* Friend, this is the greatest news! The Bible tells you to imitate God, so imitate Him. Declare, "I am going to be like God and walk in victory." This is what Ephesians 5:1 is telling you.

Realize the Victor Lives Within You

Colossians 3:12 instructs us to "put on tender mercies." Doing this is a *decision.* Imagine a person in your life who you struggle getting along with. For you to get along with this person, instead of being crushed or getting angry or building a wall around your heart, the Bible says to have tender mercies. Remember, God has tender mercies toward you, and He lives inside you.

Imitating God is like putting on your clothes. You don't have them on when you wake up — you *put them on.* This is what it is like to decide, *I'm going to put on tender mercies. It's my decision to put on tender mercies toward this person today.*

God told us to imitate Him. The One we are to imitate — the Victor — lives on the inside of us. The One who is more than a conqueror, the Holy One, dwells inside us. The Blameless One lives within us. We need to take on the identity that is truly ours and imitate God. We may not feel like it, but we can decide to put on victory right now, just as we put on tender mercies.

Remember: You are not a victim. You are more than a conqueror through Christ Jesus who loves you. Align your heart and mouth with God's Word, and walk in the victory God has given you.

STUDY QUESTIONS

Be diligent to present yourself approved to God, a worker who does not need to be ashamed, rightly dividing the word of truth.
— 2 Timothy 2:15

1. Ephesians 5:1 and 2 (*AMPC*) says, "Therefore be imitators of God [copy Him and follow His example], as well-beloved children [imi-

tate their father]. And walk in love, [esteeming and delighting in one another] as Christ loved us and gave Himself up for us, a slain offering and sacrifice to God [for you, so that it became] a sweet fragrance." According to this passage, what does it mean to imitate God?

2. Romans 8:37 tells us, "Yet in all these things we are more than conquerors through Him who loved us." To be "more than a conqueror" is to gain a decisive victory. Where do we see examples of this in the Bible? (*Consider* 1 Samuel 17:1–54; 1 Samuel 30:1–19; 2 Chronicles 20:1–25.)

3. Hebrews 12:2 says, "...Who for the joy that was set before Him, endured the cross." While Jesus was on the Cross, the joy set before Him helped Him endure the physical pain He suffered. Do you realize *you* were the joy set before Jesus while He was on the Cross?

PRACTICAL APPLICATION

**But be doers of the word,
and not hearers only, deceiving yourselves.**
—James 1:22

1. God told us to imitate Him. The One we are to imitate — the Victor — lives inside us. The Blameless One who is more than a conqueror, the Holy One, lives inside us. We need to take on the identity that is truly ours and imitate God. We may not feel like it, but we can decide to put on the Victor right now. Victors rejoice, so by faith, shout unto God with a voice *of triumph*!

2. You might have felt rejected by someone, but you are not "the rejected." That's not your identity. According to Ephesians 1:6, you are "accepted in the Beloved." *That* is your identity. You are not a victim of someone else's treatment. You are *a victor*. Take some time to bask in the truth that you are accepted *by God*. You are fully loved — by Him! Write down any insights He gives you as you meditate on this reassuring truth.

3. Do you see yourself as a victor? First Corinthians 15:57-58 says, "...Thanks be to God, who gives us the victory through our Lord Jesus Christ. Therefore, my beloved brethren, be steadfast, immovable, always abounding in the work of the Lord, knowing that your labor is not in vain in the Lord." Take time to meditate on First Corinthians 15:57 and 58 until you see yourself as a victorious child of God!

TOPIC

Are You Giving God's Way?

SCRIPTURES

1. **Ephesians 5:1** — Therefore be imitators of God as dear children.

2. **John 3:16** — For God so loved the world that He gave His only begotten Son, that whoever believes in Him should not perish but have everlasting life.

3. **John 6:12-13** — So when they were filled, He said to His disciples, "Gather up the fragments that remain, so that nothing is lost." Therefore they gathered them up, and filled twelve baskets with the fragments of the five barley loaves which were left over by those who had eaten.

4. **Matthew 5:43-48** — "You have heard that it was said, 'You shall love your neighbor and hate your enemy.' But I say to you, love your enemies, bless those who curse you, do good to those who hate you, and pray for those who spitefully use you and persecute you, that you may be sons of your Father in heaven; for He makes His sun rise on the evil and on the good, and sends rain on the just and on the unjust. For if you love those who love you, what reward have you? Do not even the tax collectors do the same? And if you greet your brethren only, what do you do more than others? Do not even the tax collectors do so? Therefore you shall be perfect, just as your Father in heaven is perfect."

5. **Romans 8:32** — He who did not spare His own Son, but delivered Him up for us all, how shall He not with Him also freely give us all things?

6. **2 Peter 1:3** — As His divine power has given to us all things that pertain to life and godliness, through the knowledge of Him who called us by glory and virtue.

7. **James 1:5** — If any of you lacks wisdom, let him ask of God, who gives to all liberally and without reproach, and it will be given to him.

8. **Lamentations 3:22** — Through the Lord's mercies we are not consumed, because His compassions fail not.

9. **Luke 6:38** — Give, and it will be given to you: good measure, pressed down, shaken together, and running over will be put into your bosom. For with the same measure that you use, it will be measured back to you.

10. **John 14:2-3** — In My Father's house are many mansions; if it were not so, I would have told you. I go to prepare a place for you. And if I go and prepare a place for you, I will come again and receive you to Myself; that where I am, there you may be also.

SYNOPSIS

God is a tremendously generous giver. He has given us His very best — His Son Jesus. He gave Him to us before we knew Him, and He gives us all we need, even when we may not deserve it. In the stories of people like Nabal and Judas, the Scriptures reveal the dangers of being stingy. But God desires that we imitate His generous nature. We are empowered to be givers like He is because His Holy Spirit lives within us.

The emphasis of this lesson:

God is the greatest of all givers! His generosity and goodness remind us that we can never outgive Him. As we imitate Him and give our very best, we will be blessed, and we will bless others in His name.

Ephesians 5:1 says, "Therefore be imitators of God as dear children." This world can try to label us as if we're victims, but Jesus was never a victim. If we're going to imitate Him, we will need to act like a victor because that's exactly who He is on the inside of us.

Another characteristic of God we can imitate is His generosity. God isn't stingy; He is always giving. As His dear children, we are called to imitate the Giver who lives within us. John 3:16 tells us, "For God so loved the world that He gave His only begotten Son, that whoever believes in Him should not perish but have everlasting life." This verse shows us how generously God gave His only begotten Son for our salvation.

God Multiplies What We Have

Another example of God's generosity could be found in John 6, which tells the amazing story of Jesus feeding the 5,000. If you know the story well, you know a boy gave his two fish and five barley loaves to feed 5,000 people. The Greek language indicates that the little boy was actually carrying small crackers along with little minnows to put on his crackers. When Jesus prayed over that tiny amount, it multiplied and multiplied.

Some scholars say that Jesus not only fed 5,000 people, but He probably fed 30,000 to 40,000 that day with just two little minnows and five small crackers. He's such a giving God! When we give God something, He doesn't just add — He multiplies! He is such a generous giver.

John 6:12 and 13 says, "So when they were filled, He said to His disciples, 'Gather up the fragments that remain, so that nothing is lost.' Therefore they gathered them up, and filled twelve baskets with the fragments of the five barley loaves which were left over by those who had eaten." In Greek, it says that the people were "filled." In certain parts of the U.S., one might say they were "stuffed to the gills." Imagine how you might feel after a large Thanksgiving meal — *that* is how much the 5,000 had eaten. They had eaten so many crackers and so many minnows that they were completely satisfied.

God Gives Generously to All

After everyone had eaten, there were so many crumbs on the ground that the leftovers filled 12 baskets. Those 12 baskets were for Jesus' 12 disciples. God had multiplied the minnows and crackers to feed the entire crowd, and there was enough left over to meet the disciples' needs too.

One of those disciples was Judas. Do you realize God gave Judas the same basketful as He gave John, Peter, James, and Andrew? God is such a giver that He even gave to His betrayer. Think of how powerful His generosity is. In Matthew 5, we see how extravagant God is in His giving. We read:

> **You have heard that it was said, 'You shall love your neighbor and hate your enemy.' But I say to you, love your enemies, bless those who curse you, do good to those who hate you, and pray for those who spitefully use you and persecute you, that you may be sons of your Father in heaven; for He makes His sun rise on the evil and on the good, and sends rain on the just and on the unjust. For if you love those who love you, what reward have you? Do not even the tax collectors do the same? And if you greet your brethren only, what do you do more than others?**

**Do not even the tax collectors do so? Therefore you shall be
perfect, just as your Father in heaven is perfect.**

— Matthew 5:43-48

God is such an amazing giver that Jesus gave a basket of crackers and
minnows to everyone who was there that day, even to His betrayer, Judas.
He shows us in His Word that we are not only to bless and love our
friends and those who love us, but our enemies and those who spitefully
use us also. This is *our* God. This is the kind of amazing giver He is.

God Gave to Us Before We Served Him

We can be glad that God gives so generously because at one point in our
life, we didn't know Jesus. Before we were saved, we weren't perfect people.
When we were dead in our sins, we didn't know God at all. We had never
done one thing for God. Even now, we may be struggling and not always
doing everything right.

But this doesn't stop God from loving us or giving to us. He is such a giver
that He made us alive in Christ Jesus. Romans 8:32 says, "He who did not
spare His own Son, but delivered Him up for us all, how shall He not with
Him also freely give us all things?" He did not spare His very best, but He
gave Him up for us all.

Sometimes we settle for giving away something we don't use anymore and
have no need for, something that is easy to give, but it is not our very best.
But God does not act that way. He gave His very best — His Son, Jesus.
Then He went even further and gave us "all things." This is how much He
loves us. He is a generous, loving Giver.

God Gives Us All We Need

God's generosity isn't limited — He abundantly provides for every aspect
of our lives. He doesn't just give enough to get by; He supplies everything
necessary for both our physical and spiritual well-being. Second Peter 1:3
says, "As His divine power has given to us all things that pertain to life
and godliness, through the knowledge of Him who called us by glory and
virtue." We are partakers of God's life. And as this verse reminds us, He
does not hold back — He gives us all we need and more.

That's why we must renew our minds. Through the knowledge of God,
we come to understand that He is not stingy. He is not withholding *from*

us; He is trying to get everything *to* us. God did not sacrifice Jesus only to withhold other blessings. No — He desires to give us "all things."

James 1:5 says, "If any of you lacks wisdom, let him ask of God, who gives to all liberally and without reproach, and it will be given to him." This verse demonstrates how, if we come to God and ask Him for wisdom, He will give it to us. The phrase "ask of God" means to *get very close to God*.

Sometimes we think drawing close to God means that we do everything perfectly. But that's not what this verse says. Rather, it indicates that we may *draw close to Him* just as we are. Our bodies are not perfect, and our minds are in the process of being renewed. But, because we accepted Jesus' into our lives and because of what He has done for us, we are perfect on the inside. Our spirits look just like Jesus.

Because of the blood of Jesus, we can take our imperfect selves and say, "God, I'm coming to You. I'm drawing near to You, Father. I'm going to talk to You as much as I can, and I will draw as close to You as possible. God, give me Your wisdom." We can draw near to the God who gives.

We Can't Outgive God

Even if we haven't been seeking Him, when we come to a situation in which we realize we need God and His wisdom, we can seek Him then. And He's such a giver! He doesn't say, "You haven't talked to Me in five years. I'm not going to do anything for you." No, that's not our God. According to His Word, He promises to give wisdom to those who seek Him. He is not the God with the clenched fist — He is the God with the open hand.

Lamentations 3:22 says, "Through the Lord's mercies we are not consumed, because His compassions fail not." Our God is such a giver that every morning, He gives to us brand-new mercies. It's as if, when we wake up, there is a package at the foot of our bed each new day — waiting for us to receive His fresh mercies.

God is the *best* Giver and a *habitual* Giver. So we ought to ask ourselves: Are we truly imitating Him as a giver? Do we only give to those who give to us, as Matthew 5 describes? Do we only give to those who love us and those who do good to us? Do we only give something we don't need and can cast away? Or do we give *our very best*?

Luke 6:38 says, "Give, and it will be given to you: good measure, pressed down, shaken together, and running over will be put into your bosom. For with the same measure that you use, it will be measured back to you." You can't outgive God — He will always give more back to you than you give Him.

Beware of the Dangers of Stinginess and Greed

We've considered how God gives generously. But what happens to those who are stingy and greedy? Think about the example in the Old Testament of Laban, the father-in-law to Jacob, who lied and cheated Jacob not just once, but over and over again (*see* Genesis 29:21-30, 30:25-31). What did greed bring to selfish Laban? Everything that Laban tried to cling to, he lost.

What about Nabal? Nabal was the husband of a beautiful woman named Abigail (*see* 1 Samuel 25). When David came seeking provision for his men, Nabal refused to give it. David grew angry, and he planned to destroy this man and those who served him. But Abigail, in all her wisdom, humility and kindness, went to David and begged for mercy. She fed him and his men. And what happened to Nabal, the stingy one? Everything he wanted to cling to, he lost — including his life.

Consider Judas. He was stingy. In the story of Mary — the sister of Martha and Lazarus — pouring out the expensive perfume and anointing the feet of Jesus, Judas rebuked her, saying she could've sold it and given the money to the poor. But he wasn't truly thinking about the poor. The Bible says he was thinking about what he could do with the money himself because he was in control of the treasury (*see* John 12:4–6). What happened to stingy Judas? He betrayed the Son of God, and he lost his life. These poignant examples beg you to consider where giving will take you versus where stinginess will take you.

God Is Preparing a Place for You

God is not a hoarder, because hoarding is all about self. Instead, God is a provider. In John 14:2 and 3, Jesus said, "In My Father's house are many mansions; if it were not so, I would have told you. I go to prepare a place for you. And if I go and prepare a place for you, I will come again and receive you to Myself; that where I am, there you may be also." Jesus declared He was going to Heaven to prepare a place for us. Even now,

He's preparing the place that He's going to one day give us, even though He has already given us so much already.

So how can we imitate God? We can't give what we don't have — God would never expect that. But we *can* give what we *do* have. Let's ask ourselves, "Am I acting stingy, or am I imitating God as a giver?

Remember Ephesians 5:1 says, "Therefore be imitators of God as dear children." We are to be imitators of God, the Giver. Can you give more of your time to people who need you? What about money, or forgiveness? Could you extend more patience or mercy? How about love? Can you choose to believe the best about someone else? What possessions can you give wholeheartedly to someone in need?

God is showing Himself to us as such a giver. He loved us when we were dead in sin, and He made us alive in Him (*see* Ephesians 2:1). His gifts are enormous, and they are working in us right now. Let's consider how we can act like God and give of ourselves or our resources today. Let's surrender ourselves to God fully, so that we can act like Him and be a wonderful giver.

We've seen the generous heart of God and the consequences of stinginess — and they are not good. But no one can outgive God. When we give, He will always give back abundantly more than we gave, so thank Him and praise Him today, because the ultimate Giver lives on the inside of you. Listen to His voice and give as He directs you. As you follow His direction you become a channel of His blessings to others. Praise God, who gives you the power to imitate Him, and live as a true giver!

STUDY QUESTIONS

Be diligent to present yourself approved to God, a worker who does not need to be ashamed, rightly dividing the word of truth.
— 2 Timothy 2:15

1. We can't give what we don't have — God would never expect that. But we *can* give what we *do* have. What do you have that you can give (your talents, time, prayers, kindness)? What else does the Bible teach us about giving? (*Consider* Matthew 5:42; Luke 6:38; and Acts 3:6.)
2. Consider where giving gets you and where stinginess gets you. Read Matthew 25:14-30, which is the parable of the talents. When it

comes to the talents the lord gave to each of his servants, what happened to the two individuals who were diligent to use their talents? What happened to the one who buried his? What does that inspire you to do with your talents and what God has entrusted you with? What does God call the people who *use* their talents?

3. God is not the God with a clenched fist — He is the God with an open hand. What do Malachi 3:10–12 and Deuteronomy 28:1–14 teach us about the blessing our giving God has for us when we obey Him?

PRACTICAL APPLICATION

But be doers of the word,
and not hearers only, deceiving yourselves.
—James 1:22

1. God is the *best* Giver, and He is a *habitual* Giver. Are you truly imitating Him, or are you only give to those who give to you? Do you just give something you don't need, or do you give *your very best*? Write down what your very best is that you can give. Ask God where you can give it and obey Him.

2. In this lesson, we explored the amazing generosity of our God. We took a look at some examples of the consequences of stinginess — and they are not good. But we have a giving God, and no matter how much we try, we can't outgive Him. When we give, He will always give back abundantly more. Take time now to praise the God who lives inside you and empowers you to be a giver!

3. Go to a place where you can be alone and take an objective look at yourself. Are you imitating God — the Giver? Ask yourself, *Am I being stingy, or am I imitating God as a giver?* If you are being stingy, make a heart adjustment and choose to imitate God and be a giver.

TOPIC

Why Should I Forgive?

SCRIPTURES

1. **Ephesians 5:1** — Therefore be imitators of God as dear children.

2. **Matthew 18:21-27** — Then Peter came to Him and said, "Lord, how often shall my brother sin against me, and I forgive him? Up to seven times?" Jesus said to him, "I do not say to you, up to seven times, but up to seventy times seven. Therefore the kingdom of heaven is like a certain king who wanted to settle accounts with his servants. And when he had begun to settle accounts, one was brought to him who owed him ten thousand talents. But as he was not able to pay, his master commanded that he be sold, with his wife and children and all that he had, and that payment be made. The servant therefore fell down before him, saying, 'Master, have patience with me, and I will pay you all.' Then the master of that servant was moved with compassion, released him, and forgave him the debt."

3. **Genesis 45:1-4** — Then Joseph could not restrain himself before all those who stood by him, and he cried out, "Make everyone go out from me!" So no one stood with him while Joseph made himself known to his brothers. And he wept aloud, and the Egyptians and the house of Pharaoh heard it. Then Joseph said to his brothers, "I am Joseph; does my father still live?" But his brothers could not answer him, for they were dismayed in his presence. And Joseph said to his brothers, "Please come near to me." So they came near. Then he said: "I am Joseph your brother, whom you sold into Egypt."

4. **Romans 5:5** — Now hope does not disappoint, because the love of God has been poured out in our hearts by the Holy Spirit who was given to us.

5. **John 17:26** — "And I have declared to them Your name, and will declare it, that the love with which You loved Me may be in them, and I in them."

6. **Acts 7:60** — Then he knelt down and cried out with a loud voice, "Lord, do not charge them with this sin." And when he had said this, he fell asleep.

7. **Luke 23:34** — Then Jesus said, "Father, forgive them, for they do not know what they do." And they divided His garments and cast lots.

SYNOPSIS

God is the ultimate Forgiver. He forgives fully and generously! We could never repay the debt of sin that we owe, but He sent Jesus to pay the price in full for us. When we are born again, He pours out His love in our hearts, empowering us to love others and forgive completely — just as He does. This great, all-encompassing forgiveness sets us free and enables us to set others free.

The emphasis of this lesson:

God, the Forgiver, lives within us. Through Him, we are empowered to *embrace* His forgiveness and *extend* it to others. In doing so, we set ourselves and others free.

Just as little children often imitate those they look up to, we are called to imitate God (*see* Ephesians 5:1). In the previous two lessons we discussed two different ways we can imitate God: by walking in victory and by being a giver. In this lesson, we will look at a third characteristic of God's that we can imitate — forgiveness.

God is an amazing forgiver. If you're born again, the blood of Jesus cleansed your slate; God does not have a ledger in Heaven listing all the bad things you've done. No matter what you've done or how much you've sinned, the blood of Jesus wiped it all away. This is the glorious forgiveness of our God. The Word of God reveals just what an amazing, complete, awesome, wonderful forgiver He is. And He calls us to imitate Him — and one of the ways we can do that is by being a forgiver.

God Forgives Us Completely

You might say, *I don't know if He forgives all my sins because some of mine are pretty bad.* It is not unusual to think this way, but it does not align with the Scriptures. We must renew our mind to the truth that God is an amazing lover and forgiver. He is a forgiving God — not a bitter God — and He wants us to imitate Him.

In the program, Denise shared a personal testimony on how she learned to imitate God's forgiving nature. You can find it below:

Many years ago, I wasn't imitating God as a forgiver. I was bitter — and bitterness was causing a disease to inhabit my body: My hands and feet were painfully cold all the time, and I was having mental struggles and panic attacks. I thought, *What is this? I'm a leader. This isn't supposed to happen to me.* I didn't know the dangers of bitterness and unforgiveness, and they were wreaking havoc in my soul and mind.

I couldn't understand it. I had already seen God as my Healer and Miracle Worker many years before this, and I knew that if He could heal me *then*, He could heal me *now*. So I sought Him diligently for the answer.

At that time, I had just ministered with Rick in a service and had just sung, yet I was still struggling. A man who was a prophet came up to me and said, "You are a very sensitive person, and you have broken places on the inside of you. But in 24 hours, you're going to wake up in a different world."

I'd been seeking God for hours every day, trying to get my heart right with Him because I knew that if I drew nearer to Him, He would draw near to me. But I was still having all those same symptoms. When this prophet spoke to me that day, I was able to speak forgiveness to someone I had been harboring unforgiveness toward. I released the individual from what had been done and asked for forgiveness.

I went to bed that night, and it was just as the prophet said. It was as if Jesus put His invisible hand down into my soul and removed the tentacles of bitterness, unforgiveness, criticism, confusion, and fear right out of my heart. When I woke up the next morning, I was completely free. My hands, feet, and mind were totally normal.

Unforgiveness and bitterness are such tormenting enemies. Perhaps you're struggling with feeling bitter. Maybe you don't even know you're in unforgiveness. You might be feeling that if a certain person would change, your life would be okay. You may not realize you are opening the door to trouble. But it's important to ask God to reveal anything hidden in your heart and make the choice to forgive whoever He might bring to your mind. We must imitate God, the ultimate Forgiver!

Close the Door to Unforgiveness

It's important to know how to imitate our God, the Forgiver. In Matthew 18:21, Jesus shares a parable of forgiveness. He tells of a master who brought in all of his servants to see what they owed him. One servant owed his master more than 1,000,000 dollars — a debt far beyond his ability to repay. Matthew 18:25–27 describes what happened next:

> **But as he was not able to pay, his master commanded that he be sold, with his wife and children and all that he had, and that payment be made. The servant therefore fell down before him, saying, "Master, have patience with me, and I will pay you all." Then the master of that servant was moved with compassion, released him, and forgave him the debt.**

What a beautiful example of how God operates! We owed Him a tremendous debt — one we could never repay. No amount of good deeds or prayers could make us acceptable to Him. Our debt of sin was too great. But Jesus came and paid that debt for us. This is what we see in Matthew 18. Through His death, Jesus forgave us completely.

Notice that the servant didn't do anything to earn it. All he did was ask, and the master forgave him. This is what happens with salvation. We first realize that we are sinners in need of our Savior and that we can't pay the debt of sin. We recognize that if we don't address our sinful nature, we're going to hell. So we come to God and say, "I believe that You are Lord. I believe that God raised You from the dead, and I confess You as my Lord. Forgive me of my sins." That's all we have to do, and in response, God washes us of all our sin. Just like the king who forgives his servant in this parable, God forgave us. This is the kind of Forgiver we have in God.

Forgiveness Creates Amazing Transformations

Great forgiveness has been shown to us. Because of the forgiveness God has demonstrated for us, we can offer that same forgiveness to others. Even when it feels difficult, remember: the Great Forgiver lives inside us.

In Genesis 45, we read about when Joseph forgave his brothers. Joseph was the son of a great man, Jacob, who had many other sons. Jacob loved

Joseph so much that he made him a coat of many colors. But Joseph's brothers became jealous so they threw him into a pit, put blood on his coat, and showed it to their father, claiming that an animal had killed Joseph. They sold their brother to the Egyptians.

Years went by, and Joseph continued to serve God. He was elevated as a servant. Then the woman of the house lied about Joseph, and the man of the house, Potiphar, threw him into prison. And while in that prison, Joseph suffered, but he never denied or rejected God. After a series of events, he was freed from that prison and became second-in-command under Pharaoh.

At that time, Joseph's family was in a bad situation because there was a famine in the land, causing Joseph to come into contact with his brothers — the same ones who lied about him, rejected him, and threw him in the pit. They had been horrible to him, and what had happened to Joseph afterward was awful. For at least 13 years, he suffered. But here he was, second-in-command under Pharaoh, and those same brothers now needed his help.

Forgiveness Is a Choice

So what did Joseph do when his brothers came to the palace? Genesis 45:1 tells us, "Then Joseph could not restrain himself before all those who stood by him, and he cried out, 'Make everyone go out from me!' So no one stood with him while Joseph made himself known to his brothers."

After revealing himself to his brothers, he could have said, "I am never going to feed you. Look what you did to me." But that is not how he chose to respond. Look at what happened in Genesis 45:2–4 as Joseph spoke to his brothers for the first time in years:

> **And he wept aloud, and the Egyptians and the house of Pharaoh heard it. Then Joseph said to his brothers, 'I am Joseph; does my father still live?' But his brothers could not answer him, for they were dismayed in his presence. And Joseph said to his brothers, 'Please come near to me.' So they came near. Then he said: 'I am Joseph your brother, whom you sold into Egypt.'**

Forgiveness is amazing. Joseph could have thrown his brothers into the dungeon or had them killed, but instead, he fed them. He fetched his father and took care of his family until they died, and they received the best land in Egypt. *That is forgiveness.*

The Power of Forgiveness

In the program, Denise shared an amazing story about another person who forgave much — the minister, Joyce Meyer. Joyce has shared publicly that her father raped her from a very early age until she left home at 18 years old. As her father became older, he needed extra care as many do when they age. Joyce didn't have to take care of him, but she became convicted in her soul about it. So she began to take care of him as well as her mother, who had never tried to protect her.

Years passed as Joyce and her husband, Dave, cared for her parents. Then one day, the phone rang — it was her mother. She told Joyce that her father had been crying all week and wanted to see her. So Joyce and Dave went to see what her father wanted. For the first time, her father admitted to what he had done and apologized to her. Then he turned to Dave and apologized to him because he knew Dave had known what he had done to Joyce — yet had shown him only kindness. Shortly after that moment, her father was baptized.

What happened to Joyce during her childhood was horrific, almost impossible to comprehend, but because of the great power of forgiveness, her father is now in Heaven with Jesus. The Forgiver lives! If you're born again, He lives in *you*. He lives in Joyce Meyer. He lives in Dave Meyer. And because the ultimate Forgiver lived inside them, Joyce and Dave were able to forgive Joyce's father, and that forgiveness paved the way for him to receive salvation and spend eternity in Heaven. That's the great power of forgiveness.

In the program, Denise shared another powerful example of forgiveness. A friend of hers in Russia had a son who struggled with drug addiction. On New Year's Eve, this woman found her son dead in her house from an overdose. Imagine being in this mother's situation. It would be easy to feel bitter, to demand justice, or seek revenge against the person who introduced her son to drugs. But instead, she chose a different path. She went to the prison where the girl who had hooked her son on drugs was imprisoned — and forgave her. Not only that, but she led the girl to Jesus. The power of God's forgiveness is such a mighty force against sin and darkness!

The Very Love of God Is in Your Heart

Only God knows everything you've been through. But through Jesus, we have all been given mercy — even though we did nothing to deserve it. If we only give people what they deserve, we will never extend mercy. If God gave us what we deserve, we would receive hell. But instead, He gave us mercy! And because He lives within us, we can imitate Him and extend that same mercy to others.

If you feel like you can't forgive someone, remember Romans 5:5: "Now hope does not disappoint, because the love of God has been poured out in our hearts by the Holy Spirit who was given to us." When forgiveness feels impossible, remind yourself that the Holy Ghost lives inside you — meaning His love and forgiveness are within you too. God's love has been shed abroad in our heart by the Holy Spirit.

Just how great is the love of God? In John 17, we see Jesus in the Garden of Gethsemane praying. In verse 26, we read the last thing He prayed to the Father while in the Garden: "And I have declared to them Your name, and will declare it, that the love with which You loved Me may be in them, and I in them."

The very love that God loved Jesus with is the same love He placed in our heart through the Holy Ghost. That means we have no excuse to say, "I can't forgive them. You don't know what they did to me!" No, we have all the equipment we need to forgive. The very love of God dwells within us, empowering us to do what seems impossible.

Don't Hold the Sins of Others Against Them

The story of Stephen, the first martyr of the church, is another amazing story of forgiveness. All he did was preach the Gospel, and the Jews grew so angry at him that they threw him out of the city, put him down in a hole, and began to stone him.

As Stephen was dying, Acts 7:60 says, "Then he knelt down and cried out with a loud voice, 'Lord, do not charge them with this sin.' And when he had said this, he fell asleep." With his last breath, he cried out, in essence, "Father, forgive them. Don't hold this against their charge." Stephen released them. Did they deserve it? No. But he gave mercy and forgave them.

What about Jesus? As He hung on the Cross, His blood poured out from every part of His body. If we had been there, even knowing Him, we wouldn't have been able to recognize Him. Jesus had every right to be bitter and angry at how He was treated — but what did He do instead? Surrounded by mockers, wracked with unimaginable pain, Jesus lifted His voice and said, "Father, forgive them, for they do not know what they do" (Luke 23:34).

According to God's Word, forgiveness means releasing the person — choosing not to hold their actions against them — or recognizing that they didn't fully understand what they were doing. God forgives, and we can, too, because the Forgiver lives within us. His love dwells in our hearts, empowering us to follow His example. Because of this, we can choose to imitate God and extend forgiveness.

Forgive Today!

You can set someone free today — and in doing so, you set yourself free. That's exactly what Denise experienced when disease imprisoned her body. She carried bitterness inside her, but when she forgave, she was set completely free — both spiritually and physically. You can experience that same freedom too.

Jesus didn't suggest that we forgive; He commanded it. As dear children of God, we are called to imitate Him. It's time to forgive.

The Word of God has cleansing power — it challenges us, strengthens us, and sets us on our feet. No matter what others have done to us, we can forgive because the Lover lives inside us. This is what God desires of us today. He wants us to imitate Him and forgive.

Take a moment to thank the Father for the presence of the Holy Spirit and the love He has shed abroad in your heart by the Holy Ghost. Right now, by your will and your words, you can choose to forgive. Think of someone you need to forgive and say, "Father, I forgive him," or "I forgive her." Be an imitator of God and set people free by the power of the Holy Ghost within you.

STUDY QUESTIONS

Be diligent to present yourself approved to God, a worker
who does not need to be ashamed, rightly dividing the word of truth.
— 2 Timothy 2:15

1. If you're born again, the blood of Jesus has washed you clean. This is the glorious forgiveness of our God. The Word of God reveals what an amazing, complete, and wonderful forgiver He is, and He calls us to imitate Him and forgive others. How can we do that even when we don't feel like it? (*Consider* Matthew 18:21-22 and Mark 11:22-25.)

2. First John 1:9 says, "If we confess our sins, He is faithful and just to forgive us our sins and to cleanse us from all unrighteousness." According to this verse, if we desire forgiveness, what do we need to do? What will God do as a result?

3. What did Jesus teach us about forgiveness in Luke 11:4? Take a moment to write your answer. How does this compare to the other scriptures we have studied on forgiveness?

PRACTICAL APPLICATION

But be doers of the word,
and not hearers only, deceiving yourselves.
— James 1:22

1. We owed God a tremendous debt — one we could never repay. No amount of good deeds or prayers could make us acceptable to Him. Our debt of sin was too great. But Jesus came and paid it for us. Through His death, Jesus forgave us. This is the kind of forgiver we have in Him. Have you accepted His forgiveness for your sins? Have you received Him as your Lord and Savior? If not, you are invited to receive Him and become born again. Simply pray this prayer from your heart: *Jesus, I believe You died on the Cross and rose from the dead. I repent of my sins. I receive You as my Lord and Savior, and I ask You to wash away my sin and make me completely new in You by Your precious blood. Thank You, Jesus! I am now redeemed. I am forgiven and filled with Your peace. In Jesus' name. Amen.*

2. Are you struggling with unforgiveness or bitterness? Realize just how great is the forgiveness God has shown you. You can give that forgiveness to others because the Forgiver lives on the inside of you. You

have been equipped with everything you need to forgive. You have the very love of God in your heart. You can pray: *Lord, please forgive me for the unforgiveness I've walked in. Cleanse me by the blood of Jesus of all bitterness and resentment. I forgive from my heart all those who have sinned against me. In Jesus' name. Amen.*

TOPIC

Are You Carrying the Fragrance of Christ?

SCRIPTURES

1. **Ephesians 5:1-2** — Therefore be imitators of God as dear children. And walk in love, as Christ also has loved us and given Himself for us, an offering and a sacrifice to God for a sweet-smelling aroma.

2. **Romans 12:1** — I beseech you therefore, brethren, by the mercies of God, that you present your bodies a living sacrifice, holy, acceptable to God, which is your reasonable service.

3. **2 Corinthians 2:14-15** — Now thanks be to God who always leads us in triumph in Christ, and through us diffuses the fragrance of His knowledge in every place. For we are to God the fragrance of Christ among those who are being saved and among those who are perishing.

4. **Genesis 8:21-22** — And the Lord smelled a soothing aroma. Then the Lord said in His heart, "I will never again curse the ground for man's sake, although the imagination of man's heart is evil from his youth; nor will I again destroy every living thing as I have done. 'While the earth remains, seedtime and harvest, cold and heat, winter and summer, and day and night shall not cease.'"

5. **Colossians 3:12-13** — Therefore, as the elect of God, holy and beloved, put on tender mercies, kindness, humility, meekness, longsuffering; bearing with one another, and forgiving one another, if anyone has a complaint against another; even as Christ forgave you, so you also must do.

SYNOPSIS

Do you realize that you carry a sweet fragrance? The Bible says you are a living sacrifice to God, and sacrifices always give off a fragrance. This sweet fragrance comes from your life and goes up to God, honoring Him. As we choose to imitate Him by consciously showing His love, mercy, and kindness to others, we spread the knowledge of who God is to those who don't know Him.

The emphasis of this lesson:

Through the Holy Spirit who dwells within us, we are supernaturally empowered to imitate God's great love. As we love others, show mercy, and act like Him, His presence fills our lives and gives off a sweet fragrance, glorifying God and drawing people closer to Him.

Think about the people you admire — whose kindness, patience, or love left a lasting impression. We often find ourselves wanting to imitate them. But as believers we're called to an even higher standard: to imitate God Himself. Ephesians 5:1 and 2 says, "Therefore be imitators of God as dear children. And walk in love, as Christ also has loved us and given Himself for us, an offering and a sacrifice to God for a sweet-smelling aroma." When Jesus went to the Cross, His death was a sacrifice to God, producing a sweet-smelling aroma. In the same way, when we walk in love toward one another, we release that same beautiful fragrance.

We Offer a Sweet Fragrance to God

When we imitate God and submit ourselves to His will, we are presenting ourselves as a living sacrifice. Romans 12:1 says, "I beseech you therefore, brethren, by the mercies of God, that you present your bodies a living sacrifice, holy, acceptable to God, which is your reasonable service." Just as Jesus' sacrifice was a sweet aroma to the Father, our lives, when surrendered to Him become a pleasing offering as well.

This aroma isn't just noticeable to God — it's noticeable to others too. In fact, it can draw people to us! Those who are not believers and don't understand the things of God may not fully understand what it is about us that stands out, but what they are sensing is the presence of God. We carry His fragrance everywhere we go. From the moment we wake up, to the places we work, study, or interact with others, we bring His presence, His fragrance with us.

We aren't just giving off a fragrance by our actions — we carry it within us because of the work God has done in our lives. Sometimes we focus too much on the natural and forget to see things through a supernatural lens. But the truth is, God has transformed us from the inside out. As Second Corinthians 5:17 says, "…if anyone is in Christ, he is a new creation." Jesus has made us holy, acceptable, and without blemish before God. Because of this, His presence within us naturally creates a fragrance that others can sense.

We Spread the Knowledge of Christ

Have you ever walked into a room and immediately noticed a pleasant fragrance? Just as a scent fills a room and lingers, our lives carry a spiritual fragrance that can affect those around us. The Bible tells us that God spreads His fragrance through us wherever we go.

Second Corinthians 2:14 says, "Now thanks be to God who always leads us in triumph in Christ, and through us diffuses the fragrance of His knowledge in every place." We can put our name into this verse and declare, "Through me, God diffuses the fragrance of His knowledge everywhere I go." Through our godly living, the fragrance of His knowledge is shared with others. It's important that we understand and believe this, because wherever we go, we are bringing the fragrance of Christ with us.

Paul continued in verses 15 and 16, explaining this idea further: "For we are to God the fragrance of Christ among those who are being saved and among those who are perishing. To the one we are the aroma of death leading to death, and to the other the aroma of life leading to life…." We bring the fragrance of the knowledge of Christ to those around us.

We're not just natural creatures; we're supernatural people filled with the power of God. Just like a fragrance diffuser spreads its scent, we carry the aroma of Christ to the world. We can boldly declare, "I am a diffuser of the knowledge of Christ. I am a diffuser of life."

We Are a Soothing Aroma to God

The first recorded sacrifice is found in Genesis 8, after the great Flood covered the earth, sparing only those aboard the Ark. When Noah stepped off the Ark, he made a sacrifice unto the Lord. Genesis 8:21 and 22 describes this pivotal moment, saying:

And the Lord smelled a soothing aroma. Then the Lord said in His heart, 'I will never again curse the ground for man's sake, although the imagination of man's heart is evil from his youth; nor will I again destroy every living thing as I have done. "While the earth remains, seedtime and harvest, cold and heat, winter and summer, and day and night shall not cease."'

When Noah made his sacrifice, it became a sweet aroma to the Lord. In fact, the aroma was so pleasing that the Lord gave many promises, and He has kept them to this day. Take a moment to imagine that scene: Noah offering up his sacrifice in gratitude, a love exchange between man and Creator.

Think back on everything God had done up to that moment. He had saved Noah and his family, sparing them from the destruction of millions. Can you imagine hearing the screams of the people, crying, "Noah, open the door! We're perishing. We're drowning!" But the door remained shut because God had sealed it. Picture the torrential waves, crashing and sweeping everything away as the Ark remained afloat.

After 40 days in the Ark, Noah and his family finally stepped out, the only eight survivors in the world. Imagine that — God saving you from such a fate. It's no surprise that Noah set aside time to offer a sacrifice of thanksgiving to God for His mercy. The aroma of his sacrifice was so wonderful to God that He promised to never destroy the world by water again!

Let Your Love Be a Sacrifice

When you offer appreciation for everything the Lord has done for you, it brings a pleasant aroma to God. Never underestimate the power of your worship and praise. As you live your life for Him, you are becoming a living sacrifice.

Forgiveness can be a sacrifice, especially when it's difficult. You may even find yourself having to forgive someone over and over. You're called to love those who may be difficult to love or those who seem unlovable. The Bible asks us, "But if you love those who love you, what credit is that to you?" (Luke 6:32–34). Even sinners do that. But when we love those who spitefully use us or curse us, and we bless them instead, we are embodying the true love of God. In doing this, we offer ourselves as living sacrifices — and it brings a sweet-smelling aroma before God.

Remember, we are not just natural people — we are supernatural, empowered by God's presence. As His children, we are a diffuser of His presence and His knowledge. When we walk in love toward one another, we're imitating God, just as Ephesians 5:1 says: "Therefore be imitators of God as dear children."

Put On the Mercy of God

Maybe you struggle with imitating God. You might say, "I still don't know how I can imitate God." Colossians 3:12 reveals how you can do so: "Therefore, as the elect of God, holy and beloved, put on tender mercies, kindness, humility, meekness, longsuffering." The beginning of this verse points to those who are "the elect of God, holy and beloved." That's who *you* are. You are the holy and beloved elect of God. And as the holy and beloved elect of God, you are to *put on* tender mercies, kindness, humility, meekness, and longsuffering.

When you got up this morning, you didn't already have on your day clothes. No, you had to put each item of clothing on one by one. In the same way, if you want to be a living sacrifice to the Lord, you must *put on* tender mercies, kindness, humility, meekness, and longsuffering.

Look at the first among this list — tender mercies. God has been so merciful to us even though we didn't deserve mercy. If God were to give us what we deserved, we would receive hell at the end of our life — because that's what we *deserve*. We deserve judgment, but God gave us mercy instead. Because of His great mercy, Jesus now lives in us by the Holy Spirit and has given us the power to be living sacrifices. And because He lives inside us, we can put on tender mercies and offer mercy to someone else.

What about kindness? When we give kindness to someone, we are being a living sacrifice. We are an aroma to God. In addition to putting on tender mercies and kindness, Colossians 3:12 and 13 informs us we are to put on "…humility, meekness, longsuffering; bearing with one another, and forgiving one another.…" This means we need to give grace to one another. And when we give grace to one another, we forgive one another. We're being a living sacrifice to Him, bringing that sweet aroma to the Lord.

Diffuse the Knowledge of God

Because God is within us, we become diffusers of the knowledge and presence of Christ (*see* 2 Corinthians 2:14). Think of a diffuser for a moment.

A diffuser has perfume on the inside, and when it's activated by the fire of electricity, it releases a fragrance into the air. In the same way, when the fire of the Holy Spirit moves in us, He brings out the sweet fragrance of Christ's love and presence.

When we allow the fire of the Holy Spirit to touch us and agree with Him, God's fragrance becomes powerful. We can choose to forgive, to show mercy, and walk in God's love. We are not simply living naturally; we are living supernaturally, empowered by the Holy Spirit. And this supernatural love is recognized by the world around us.

Every morning, we can make the decision to rise and declare, "I'm not just struggling through life. I've got the power of the Holy Spirit in me, and I am a diffuser of His knowledge. I am a diffuser of life to the living. I am a diffuser of conviction to the lost." This is the power that resides within us, and we are called to acknowledge and walk in it.

By using our faith, we choose to imitate God. Even when we don't feel like forgiving, when we don't feel like showing mercy, we can say, "I recognize the power within me, and I choose to act in love, just as God does." In doing so, we are diffusing the presence and knowledge of Christ to everyone we encounter, spreading His life and His love.

Recognize Who You Truly Are

First Corinthians 7:14 tells us that a believing spouse can sanctify an unbelieving spouse. How is that possible? It's possible because, as believers, we carry the presence of Christ within us. Even if our spouse is not saved, our very presence as a diffuser of Christ's knowledge and life can have a transforming effect on them.

Let's begin to recognize who we truly are in Christ. Let's become imitators of God as dear children and walk in the love that He's given us. Remember, Ephesians 5:1 and 2 says, "Therefore be imitators of God as dear children. And walk in love, as Christ also has loved us and given Himself for us, an offering and a sacrifice to God for a sweet-smelling aroma."

When Jesus gave His life, His sacrifice was a sweet aroma to God. Similarly, as Romans 12:1 says, you are to "present your bodies a living sacrifice." As a living sacrifice, you are giving a sweet aroma to God. Even right now, with Christ in you, you are releasing a pleasing fragrance to this lost world and to every believer. You are powerful, and you are supernatural. Expect the supernatural to flow through you!

STUDY QUESTIONS

Be diligent to present yourself approved to God, a worker
who does not need to be ashamed, rightly dividing the word of truth.
— 2 Timothy 2:15

1. When we love as God loves, we diffuse the fragrance of Christ to those around us. What else does the Bible teach us about walking in the love of God? (*Consider* 1 Corinthians 13:4-8 *AMPC*); Galatians 5:22; and 1 John 2:5.)

2. Noah obeyed God by building the Ark. Once he, his family, and all the animals were in the Ark, God sealed the door shut. Have you ever done what God told you to do, and when you did, something supernatural happened? That's what happened with Noah, and the same can happen to you. Obey God and trust Him to show up and do what only He can do. (*Consider* Isaiah 1:19 and Exodus 24:7.)

3. As Denise mentioned in the program, we are to put on tender mercies. God has been merciful to us even though we didn't deserve it. We deserve judgment, but God gave us mercy instead. Because of His great mercy, Jesus now lives in us by the Holy Spirit. Because we have Jesus inside us, we can put on tender mercies and offer it to someone else. What does God's Word tell us about the His tender mercies? (*Consider* Psalm 103:4; Psalm 145:9; and Lamentations 3:22-23.)

PRACTICAL APPLICATION

But be doers of the word,
and not hearers only, deceiving yourselves.
— James 1:22

1. Wherever we go, we are bringing the fragrance of Christ with us. We're not just natural creatures — we're supernatural people with the power of God inside us! Because we have the Holy Spirit within us, we've become like a fragrance diffuser. By faith, say this about yourself: *I am a diffuser of the knowledge of Christ. I am a diffuser of life.* That is the truth!

2. There are specific things the Bible tells us to "put on." Colossians 3:12 and 13 tells us to *put on* "…tender mercies, kindness, humility, meekness, longsuffering; bearing with one another and forgiving one another…." When we put these things on, we're being living sacrifices and releasing that sweet aroma to God. Intentionally take a few minutes to "put on" what Colossians 3:12 and 13 instructs and renew your mind toward your family, friends, coworkers, neighbors, and those who surround you.

3. We deserve judgment, but God gave us mercy and love. Now we have the power to put on that same love and give it to someone else. Use your faith and imitate God by consecrating yourself to walk in love toward those who have been difficult to love in the past. As you do, you are diffusing Christ's presence and life!

LESSON 5

TOPIC

Are You Ready To Let Go of Worry?

SCRIPTURES

1. **Ephesians 5:1-2** — Therefore be imitators of God as dear children. And walk in love, as Christ also has loved us and given Himself for us, an offering and a sacrifice to God for a sweet-smelling aroma.

2. **Romans 12:1** — I beseech you therefore, brethren, by the mercies of God, that you present your bodies a living sacrifice, holy, acceptable to God, which is your reasonable service.

3. **Psalm 2:4** — He who sits in the heavens shall laugh; the Lord shall hold them in derision.

4. **Revelation 4:4-6** — Around the throne were twenty-four thrones, and on the thrones I saw twenty-four elders sitting, clothed in white robes; and they had crowns of gold on their heads. And from the throne proceeded lightnings, thunderings, and voices. Seven lamps of fire were burning before the throne, which are the seven Spirits of God. Before the throne there was a sea of glass, like crystal. And in the midst of the throne, and around the throne, were four living creatures full of eyes in front and in back.

5. **Matthew 6:25-27** — Therefore I say to you, do not worry about your life, what you will eat or what you will drink; nor about your body, what you will put on. Is not life more than food and the body more than clothing? Look at the birds of the air, for they neither sow nor reap nor gather into barns; yet your heavenly Father feeds them. Are you not of more value than they? Which of you by worrying can add one cubit to his stature?

6. **1 Peter 5:7** — Casting all your care upon Him, for He cares for you.

7. **Colossians 3:15** — And let the peace of God rule in your hearts, to which also you were called in one body; and be thankful.

8. **Philippians 4:6** — Be anxious for nothing, but in everything by prayer and supplication, with thanksgiving, let your requests be made known to God.

9. **Hebrews 12:14** — Pursue peace with all people, and holiness, without which no one will see the Lord.

SYNOPSIS

God is not a worrier, and as His dear children, we are to imitate Him. Throughout the Bible, we find encouragement and instruction on why we should not worry — because worrying does not serve us. When we worry, we hinder what God can do in our lives. But when we choose to trust Him, we create space for Him to move, bringing His peace that surpasses all understanding (*see* Philippians 4:7) into our lives.

The emphasis of this lesson:

Our unshakeable God is not moved by anything that happens in our world — and we do not need to be moved either. Our born-again spirit is not filled with worry, but rather with trust and reliance on God. As we lean on Him, His peace saturates our lives, and we are empowered to live above the cares of this world.

In the last several lessons, we have discussed how we are to "be imitators of God" (*see* Ephesians 5:1). The phrase "be imitators of God" means *to act just like Him*. How do we act like Him? The next verse gives us the answer, and it has a lot to do with our attitude: "And walk in love, as Christ also has loved us and given Himself for us, an offering and a sacrifice to God for a sweet-smelling aroma" (v. 2).

To imitate God, we must first look at His example — Jesus. When we look at Jesus' life on the earth, we can see that He was always a victor, never the victim. Only He had the power to lay down His life for us — not the devil, not man. Because Jesus is always victorious, we are always victorious — that's who we are!

We also learned that Jesus is a giver; He's never stingy. He gave His life as a sacrifice, and now we, too, can become true givers. He is also a forgiver. Forgiveness is a powerful force! God forgave us and showed us mercy even though we didn't deserve it. And because He forgave us, we can now forgive others.

Ephesians 5:2 says that when Jesus gave His life for us, it was "a sacrifice to God for a sweet-smelling aroma." Just like Jesus, when we obey God and submit ourselves to His will, we release a fragrance and become "living sacrifices" (*see* Romans 12:1). But these aren't the only characteristics we can imitate from God.

God Is Not Worried

We talked about how God is a giver, a victor, and a forgiver throughout this study guide. Guess what? God is also not a worrier; He never worries. He's not even worried right now, neither was He worried yesterday. Many years ago, there was a popular song that said, "Don't worry, be happy." There is a lot of truth to that song because to worry takes away our peace. If we're going to be imitators of God, then we need to take on this characteristic of God and not be a worrier.

Throughout the Bible, we find encouragement and instruction on how we can avoid worrying. Nothing is impossible with God, and we have the power of the Holy Spirit within us. With the help of the Holy Spirit, we can become someone who doesn't worry, but who trusts and rests in and is overcome by the peace of God. To illustrate this idea, Denise shared a testimony from her own life.

A few years ago, Denise was upset and worried about several things. She and her husband Rick were traveling, taking one airplane after another, and holding many meetings. And while Denise is used to the busyness of travel, especially when they travel in the U.S., this particular time too many things were going on at once. So she talked to God about it. He said, "Denise, I'm not worried or upset. I'm completely peaceful about this." Those words really comforted Denise. Even though she was worrying, God wasn't — He was at peace.

Similarly, things may be going on in your life or around you. You may be wondering, *What is going to happen? What will happen to me and my family?* All the what-ifs come up, and it seems as if everything is crashing down on your mind, emotions, or body. So how can you stand against worry? Remind yourself that God is not worried about your situation. He has it all under control. Since we are to "be imitators of God" (*see* Ephesians 5:1), we can act like God by not worrying about our situation either.

God Is Our Unshakeable Fortress

Not only is God not worried about our lives or situations, He is also untroubled by governmental, political, or economic issues. When we reflect on what's happening in the world, we can draw comfort from the truth that God is unshakable — He is our rock, our fortress, and He never changes.

Psalm 2:4 says, "He who sits in the heavens shall laugh; the Lord shall hold them in derision." God is not impressed by the power of evil men. He is the one who gives them the very breath that they breathe, even if they fail to acknowledge Him. Without His provision, they wouldn't survive for a moment.

If God didn't sustain the world "by the word of His power" (Hebrews 1:3), everything would fall apart. He is holding all things together. It doesn't matter what mankind believes about their power, technology, or genius; they couldn't even think or see without God enabling them to do so.

In other words, God is working in ways we can't always see. We may not give Him credit for all He does, but even so, He's working behind the scenes and shaking things up. He's holding everything together, and yet He is not worried. And because the Holy Spirit lives within us, we are called to imitate Him — by choosing trust over worry. Revelation 4:4–6 reminds us:

> **Around the throne were twenty-four thrones, and on the thrones I saw twenty-four elders sitting, clothed in white robes; and they had crowns of gold on their heads. And from the throne proceeded lightnings, thunderings, and voices. Seven lamps of fire were burning before the throne, which are**

the seven Spirits of God. Before the throne there was a sea of glass, like crystal. And in the midst of the throne, and around the throne, were four living creatures full of eyes in front and in back.

Does this verse give the impression that God is sitting on the throne worrying? No, friend, God is not worried; He's not a worrier. Through the Holy Spirit, He gives us the power to refuse the spirit of worry. And we can be imitators of Him!

Worrying Does Nothing To Help Us

In Matthew 6:25 and 26, Jesus instructed us to not worry. He said, "Therefore I say to you, do not worry about your life, what you will eat or what you will drink; nor about your body, what you will put on. Is not life more than food and the body more than clothing? Look at the birds of the air, for they neither sow nor reap nor gather into barns; yet your heavenly Father feeds them. Are you not of more value than they?"

This is such a powerful verse. If God takes care of the birds and the ants, then wouldn't He also take care of us? Are we not more valuable than a bird? Of course we are. Verse 27 goes on to say, "Which of you by worrying can add one cubit to his stature?" Worrying does nothing for us. In fact, it only brings misfortune to us! It causes us to become older more quickly, it can cause disease in our body, it's a waste of our mental and emotional energy, and it can cause us to put a guard around ourselves against other people.

Worry is not a part of our born-again spirit — our trust and our reliance on God *is*. We are not meant to be worriers; we're meant to trust and rest in God. And Ephesians 5:1 says, we are to "…be imitators of God as dear children." Dare to imitate the One who is on the inside of you, the One who's not worried, and you also will not be worried.

Imitating God Takes Faith

It takes faith to imitate God and declare, "I am not going to worry about this one more second. God is not worried about it, so I'm not worried about it." When we agree with what's on the inside of us, we open up a place for God to move in our situation. When we worry, it's as if we have our hands on the situation, refusing to give it to God. We try and try to figure it out on our own. We think, *If I can just do this…. If that person will stop doing that.... What if this happens? What if...?* If we worry, worry, worry, then *we're* in control — not God.

But when we trust God, we allow Him to come into the situation and do something amazing. This is such great news. Remember, God takes care of even the birds. Are you not much more valuable than a bird? He is watching you and He is working behind the scenes in your situation, right this very minute!

There is a song that goes, "His eye is on the sparrow." Friend, God's eye is on *you*. First Peter 5:7 says, "Casting all your care upon Him, for He cares for you." If we take hold of our cares and worries, we're ignoring that God cares for us. He is calling us to look at His Word and realize that He has not called us to live in worry. We aren't to be like the world and be filled with worry and complaints. Instead we are to trust Him.

Let His Peace Rule in Your Heart

God doesn't want us to let worry rule our thoughts. No. In fact, Colossians 3:15 says, "And let the peace of God rule in your hearts, to which also you were called in one body; and be thankful." Instead of allowing worry and fear to rule our hearts and minds, we are to let the peace of God rule. We need to decide to be an imitator of the non-worrying God who lives on the inside of us. We have the power to choose to use our faith, refuse to worry, and allow the peace of God to dominate our lives.

The peace of God is so powerful! When we open up to the peace of God, it acts as an umpire in our lives. If we yield to the peace of God, it will put a stop to worry. His peace says, "Worry, you can't come in here. Strife, you can't come in here. Stay out, confusion. This is a place of peace."

Philippians 4:6 says, "Be anxious for nothing, but in everything by prayer and supplication, with thanksgiving, let your requests be made known to God." Amazingly, this verse was written when the apostle Paul was in a horrible prison. If anybody had a reason to worry, it would have been Paul. He was surrounded by sewage in this particular prison, and death was all around him. But what did Paul write about instead? He wrote, "Be anxious for nothing."

The word "nothing" means, *Don't be anxious about the tiniest, smallest detail.* So what does this verse instruct us to do? We are to act like God and not worry.

The verse goes on to say, "…But in everything by prayer and supplication, with thanksgiving.…" Supplication is talking to God, pouring out our heart about the matter. He wants to hear from us about our situation, along with our thanksgiving. Then the verse adds, "…Let your request be made known unto God." When we give our problems over to the Lord, we set ourselves up to be surrounded by the peace of God, which surpasses all understanding.

Pursue His Peace

We are the fragrance of God to the world. When things are going wrong, and yet we trust in God, the peace we will experience will be beyond our understanding. People may even notice and say, "I don't understand how you can be so peaceful." When we cast our worries over on the Lord, the power of the Holy Spirit within us produces that amazing peace. We have the very power we need to be an imitator of God — to not worry, but to walk in peace.

Hebrews 12:14 says, "Pursue peace with all people, and holiness, without which no one will see the Lord." The word "pursue" means *to actively chase after something*, similar to hunting an animal down. When we hunt something down, we do it *on purpose*. Some hunters camouflage them-selves and sit in trees for hours, not saying a word as they wait for their prey. When these hunters do catch their prey, it's not by accident; they did it on purpose. In the same way, we can imitate God by choosing to pursue peace.

When we actively pursue God's peace and cast our cares on Him, we are being an imitator of God. We are fulfilling Ephesians 5:1: "Therefore be imitators of God as dear children." We imitate Him by saying no to worry and choosing to trust in Him.

Friend, you're more powerful than you realize. Your born-again spirit car-ries no worry — rather, it carries faith, love, and God's surpassing peace. Agree with the truth of God's Word, act on it, and you will imitate God by being one who doesn't worry. The Holy Spirit within you empowers you to walk free of worry and anxiety, and to be someone who trusts God fully, casting every care on Him.

The world is overwhelmed with worry, fear, and anxiety like never before. So many people take medication to treat their anxiety and fear as a way to calm down. But you don't have to live like that. God's peace is already within you. You have the power to rise above worry, to stand firm in faith, and to live in the supernatural peace that only God can give. Let's be imitators of God and resist worry, standing in victory, forgiveness, and peace.

STUDY QUESTIONS

Be diligent to present yourself approved to God, a worker
who does not need to be ashamed, rightly dividing the word of truth.
— 2 Timothy 2:15

1. Dare to imitate the One who is on the inside of you, the One who's not worried. By putting your full trust in God and casting your cares on Him, you will find His all-surpassing peace. Read Luke 12:22-32. What perspective does this passage bring to any area you've been tempted to worry about lately?

2. Hebrews 12:14 says, "Pursue peace with all people, and holiness, without which no one will see the Lord." We can imitate God by choosing to pursue peace on purpose. What else does the Bible teach us about peace? (*Consider* Psalm 34:14; 1 Thessalonians 5:23; and 2 Timothy 2:22.)

3. Peace and rest are the opposite of worry. What does Matthew 11:28-30 tell us to do if we "labor and are heavy laden"?

PRACTICAL APPLICATION

But be doers of the word,
and not hearers only, deceiving yourselves.
— James 1:22

1. Imitating God takes faith. It takes faith to declare, "I am not going to worry about this one more second. God is not worried about it, so I'm not worried about it." Choose to use your faith, refuse to worry, and allow the peace of God to rule in your heart. Take time to release your faith now regarding a situation you've been tempted to worry about. By faith, take time to praise God for the answer.

2. The Bible is filled with encouragement and instruction on how we can avoid worrying. We have the power of the Holy Ghost on the inside of us. Nothing is impossible with God, and we can become someone who isn't worrying, but who trusts and rests in and is overcome by the peace of God. Do you know others who need the truths in this lesson?

Contact them and share with them something from this valuable lesson.

3. Arm yourself with the Word of God so that the next time you are faced with a challenging circumstance, you'll cast the care on the Lord rather than worry about it. Take time to read over the verses at the beginning of the lesson and then meditate on the one you need the most. Watch what God will do as you put His Word into practice and imitate Him by not worrying!

A Prayer To Receive Salvation

If you've never received Jesus as your Savior and Lord, now is the time for you to experience the new life Jesus wants to give you! To receive God's gift of salvation that can be obtained through Jesus alone, pray this prayer from your heart:

> *Jesus, I repent of my sin and receive You as my Savior and Lord. Wash away my sin with Your precious blood and make me completely new. I thank You that my sin is removed, and Satan no longer has any right to lay claim on me. Through Your empowering grace, I faithfully promise that I will serve You as my Lord for the rest of my life.*

If you just prayed this prayer of salvation, you are born again! You are a brand-new creation in Christ! Would you please let us know of your decision by going to **renner.org/salvation**? We would love to connect with you and pray for you as you begin your new life in Christ.

Scriptures for further study: John 3:16; John 14:6; Acts 4:12; Ephesians 1:7; Hebrews 10:19,20; 1 Peter 1:18,19; Romans 10:9,10; Colossians 1:13; 2 Corinthians 5:17; Romans 6:4; 1 Peter 1:3

Notes

CLAIM YOUR FREE RESOURCE!

As a way of introducing you further to the teaching ministry of Rick Renner, we would like to send you FREE of charge his teaching, "How To Receive a Miraculous Touch From God" on CD or as an MP3 download.

How To Receive
a Miraculous Touch From God
Rick Renner

CD36

RENNER

In His earthly ministry, Jesus commonly healed *all* who were sick of *all* their diseases. In this profound message, learn about the manifold dimensions of Christ's wisdom, goodness, power, and love toward all humanity who came to Him in faith with their needs.

☑ **YES, I want to receive Rick Renner's monthly teaching letter!**

Simply scan the QR code to claim this resource or go to:
renner.org/claim-your-free-offer

Connect

WITH US!

🏠 renner.org

f facebook.com/rickrenner • facebook.com/rennerdenise

▶ youtube.com/rennerministries • youtube.com/deniserenner

📷 instagram.com/rickrrenner • instagram.com/rennerministries_
instagram.com/rennerdenise

www.ingramcontent.com/pod-product-compliance
Lightning Source LLC
Chambersburg PA
CBHW071650040426
42452CB00009B/1826

* 9 7 8 1 6 6 7 5 1 2 3 7 2 *